CW00839952

Reflections on the Life and Thought of

BLAISE PASCAL

A RHYMED RESPONSE

Reflections on the Life and Thought of

BLAISE PASCAL

A RHYMED RESPONSE

ROSALIND HENDERSON

PIMPERNEL
PRESS LTD
www.pimpernelpress.com

Pimpernel Press Limited
www.pimpernelpress.com

Reflections on the Life and Thought of Blaise Pascal
A Rhymed Response
© Pimpernel Press Limited 2017
Text © Rosalind Henderson 2017

Rosalind Henderson has asserted her right to be identified as the author
of this work in accordance with the Copyright, Designs and Patents Act
1988 (UK).

All rights reserved. No part of this publication may be reproduced,
stored in a retrieval system or transmitted, in any form, or by any means,
electronic, mechanical, photocopying, recording or otherwise, without
prior permission in writing from the publisher or a licence permitting
restricted copying. In the United Kingdom such licences are issued by the
Copyright Licensing Agency, Barnard's Inn, 86 Fetter Lane,
London EC4A 1EN.

A catalogue record for this book is available from the British Library.

Designed by Becky Clarke
Typeset in Adobe Garamond

ISBN 978-1-910258-85-9
Printed and bound in the United Kingdom at Berforts Ltd
9 8 7 6 5 4 3 2 1

COVER ILLUSTRATION: *Blaise Pascal*. A drawing in red chalk by Domat,
a friend of Pascal's – the only portrait of Pascal made while he was alive.
(Photo by Culture Club/Getty Images)

CONTENTS

PREFACE

As historian David Wootton[1] has reminded us, Voltaire is said to have read Pascal obsessively, although he hated him. I too have read him obsessively for most of my adult life. My admiration is not that of a mathematician or philosopher, or even that of a fellow believer, but because I recognise that I belong to the same human family, whose aspirations are thwarted by weakness, whose noble intentions are muddied by selfishness, and who feel ever more disorientated by the revelations of science and insignificant in the vastness of the universe.

I put together the 'rhymed response' initially for the purposes of a French literature class, as an easily read introduction to the life and work of Pascal. Using Alban Krailsheimer's Penguin translation of the Lafuma edition of the *Pensées* – in which form I have always read them – I wrote verse to suggest ways in which his thoughts would have been received in the seventeenth century, and how they could be received by modern readers, with the intention of encouraging students to voice their own response. It was because I admired Pascal's terse, condensed style that I felt poetry to be the best representation; following Pascal's lead, I have responded with different voices, choosing for some the poetic style of his contemporaries (and in two instances the flippant tone that might have been taken by the brilliant young scientist himself, or his admirers, in reaction to the pompous verbiage of the Establishment). Further in the book I have chosen to show the possible response of people of our generation.

1 BBC Radio 4, 'In Our Time', 19 September 2013.

I am indebted to a number of scholars whose studies have provided reliable documentation of his life and analysis of his thought. A full account of Pascal's life can be read in Alban Krailsheimer's study in the Past Masters series or in his revised introduction to the recent Penguin editions; and also in *Pascal* by Jean Steinmann, translated by Martin Turnell. While writing this, I have been introduced to the masterly commentary by Peter Kreeft. *Christianity for Modern Pagans* persuades, in exciting and convincing prose, that there is a need to rediscover the wisdom of the *Pensées* and consider their relevance to the problems facing our own age. I have taken the liberty of quoting extensively from this book.

In *Pascal*, Steinmann comments, 'The many editions of the *Pensées* and the very diversity of their classifications confirm the incomplete nature of the book and the freedom left to everybody to read them in their own way.' I hope I may be encouraging my readers to do the same.

I

THE EARLY YEARS

Pascal was born on 19 June 1623, at Clermont in Auvergne. Only three years later his mother died and his father was left to bring up Blaise and his two sisters, Gilberte and Jacqueline. Pascal was not a healthy child, and much of his education was carried out at home. His father, who was himself well versed in mathematics and science, encouraged his son to pursue these studies, and the first fruits of Blaise's creative spirit were the calculating machine and other apparatuses for solving arithmetical problems. The calculating machine, built in 1644 by craftsmen in the city of Rouen, where the family was then living, is often considered the progenitor of the computer. It is just one of the many feats of the young polymath for which he is remembered by mathematicians and scientists. At this time he was also working on theories of probability and problems in gaming, both of which would feature again in later life.

In 1646 he addressed the then controversial issue of the existence of vacuum – a matter that divided churchmen as well as scientists. In 1644 the physicist Torricelli had set up experiments using columns of mercury which he took up a tower, and Pascal chose to repeat these on the summit of the local Auvergne mountain, the Puy de Dôme. Pascal's series of experiments typify the method he adopted throughout his life: he could never let an idea go unchallenged by experience or by common sense and, unlike Descartes, he did not believe one could arrive at knowledge through reason alone. 'Does the theory work in practice?' we see him asking when investigating the deepest preoccupations of humanity. Reason must cohere with intuition.

In seventeenth-century views and laws
Vacuum is what nature most abhors.
So, up the Puy de Dôme our hero goes,
And his superior grasp of science shows:
The tube of mercury can prove
That when the level drops
There's space above.
And if your eyes can see there's nothing there,
Don't complicate it all
With talk of weightless air.

2

REVELATION

IN THAT SAME YEAR, 1646, Pascal's life started to take a new direction. The two doctors who were called in to apply their skills to an injury sustained by Pascal's father, turned out to be devotees of Jansenism, a movement that called for more reforms than the Counter-Reformation had yet produced in the Catholic Church. Their earnest demeanour and ardent spirituality made converts of the whole family. Jacqueline, the younger sister, gave up her interest in the theatre to enter the convent of Port-Royal, a centre of Jansenist devotion.

Pascal's life did not undergo quite so dramatic a change at this stage. His real conversion occurred suddenly on the night of 23 November 1654, when he received a revelation that changed his whole attitude to life. The God of Abraham, Isaac and Jacob was presented to him in fiery certitude, and brought unspeakable joy, as it became apparent to him that this God was also the God of Jesus Christ.

The experience not only confirmed his faith; it highlighted the difference between this faith and the vague deistic philosophy of Descartes. He wrote that deism – which eschewed revelation, and held that the existence of God could be assured by reason and observation – was as remote from Christianity as atheism. No less remote was the agnosticism entertained by Montaigne and his followers. Montaigne is known for his collection of essays expressing scepticism or, more correctly, Pyrrhonism – a suspension of judgement. He is said to have struck a medal inscribed 'What do I know?' Pascal was always prepared to see the value of keeping an open mind, but he condemned the self-indulgence that this appeared to justify. At the other end of the scale, many followers of the principles of Stoicism tried to persuade themselves that, with a determined effort, men could gain mastery of themselves and of the world. Epictetus, a freed slave, who died about AD 125, had written a manual offering a concise statement of practical Stoicism, which became very popular with the *honnêtes hommes* (men of noble ideals) of Pascal's time. Pascal saw that this philosophy was gaining adherents, and recognised that it ran contrary to a gospel of a God involved historically and actually in human affairs.

The Memorial, as he called the record of his revelatory experience, he kept folded with him in an inner pocket for the rest of his life. It was not found until after his death, and was probably not intended for inclusion in the Apologia which he started working on in later years.

The Memorial

Memorial night of exultation
Found him deep in contemplation
Of the God of all creation.
Fire not set for conflagration;
Joy beyond all jubilation
Brought his faith its confirmation.

So sure and startling a revelation
Toppled the tower of Descartes' cogitation;
Shattered the Stoics' self-congratulation;
Agnostics' lazy prevarication.
Restored the role of adoration
To God's masterpiece in his creation
Such elation!

On that crystalline night of fire
You met the really real,
The truly true,
The eternally present;

Saw indubitably stated
In flames of joy,
With the cold precision
Of a mathematical solution
The reason of being.
The crystalline experience of your night of fire
Clinched it for you:
Disbanded Descartes
And his cogitation
In favour of exploration;
Dispelled Montaigne's not ignoble doubt
Adopted in humility;
Dispelled far more the amorality
Condoned in his perplexity.
Epictetus, stoic bold
(Claiming for sure we're on our own
Gritting his teeth and battling on
Heaven cold-shouldered, standing proudly alone),
Must be told.

3

THE WORLD OR THE CLOISTER?

Shortly after their encounter with the Jansenists, the Pascal family moved to Paris. There Blaise, still in his twenties, became immersed in the new science, born with the discoveries of Galileo, and the new philosophy, initiated by Descartes. Pascal soon made his name in both of these domains. More significant with regard to the *Pensées* were his friendships with the aristocratic circle of the *honnêtes hommes*, cultivated men of all-round excellence and noble ideals who could be counted upon to behave honourably; Montaigne is considered to exemplify them. Montaigne's inoffensive agnosticism, which resulted from a careful scrutiny of human nature, and the conclusion that we are unalterably what we are, resulted in an uncritical and, to some extent, cynical lifestyle. These men of integrity offered much to admire, but Pascal noted that they opted to turn away from the serious questions facing the human situation. It was during these years that the idea began to form for an Apologia, or defence, of his faith. He so much wanted to show his friends that the happiness they sought and the way to self-fulfilment were to be found in God alone.

Port-Royal became a sort of beacon. Pascal taught there for a while, and had a pupil in his class who became a leading playwright and whose dramas demonstrated the effects of unbridled passion – Jean Racine. He continued his association with the laymen who were attached to the community – *les messieurs* – and treasured the closer link he now had through his sister. Compared with the calm life of prayer he experienced there, the busy bustle of life at the court of Louis XIV would have seemed very alien, but Pascal appears not to have considered taking holy orders himself. He was an observer with other gifts for the world.

At Port-Royal

To see the fate of the headstrong heart
I turn to Port-Royal,
Where sisters seek no heaven haven,
But, dignified at the world's window,
Channel their prayer to its turbulent needs;
Where Jean Racine sits head in hands
And pens his *Phèdre*, lost to lust;
Where Blaise himself,
Not strong in body
But strong enough in soul
To ride the stormy seas,
To guide the searching of poor hearts
When grace, an anchor they have cast adrift,
Passes unrecognised.
Those who through passion blind
Know only tossing of the waves
Can then, like James and John,
Implore you, Lord, to save;
Call out across the sea,
'Help us, O Saviour, or we drown.'

4

THE HEART HAS ITS REASONS
THAT REASON KNOWS NOT OF

OBSERVING THE SHORT-LIVED ENTHUSIASMS AND INFATUATIONS of his Paris friends, recalling the intuitional flashes and insights that had driven his scientific enquiry and, above all, remembering his night of revelation, Pascal concluded that the mind works on two different levels. He termed these *l'esprit de géométrie* and *l'esprit de finesse*, which we may consider as the rational and inspirational. He could be seen to be reaching into the future with this analysis, if one compares it with the studies of religious experience made by William James in the late nineteenth century, but he was also reaching back to Augustine and reaching across to Protestant theology.

Little wonder that he was regarded with suspicion, especially by the Jesuits, firm upholders of the status quo. The Society of Jesus, operating under a general and with royal connections (Henri IV took a Jesuit confessor after his conversion to Catholicism), was a match for Calvinism in its absolute commitment to advancing its cause (the historian G.R.R. Treasure views them as 'equipped to fight for the souls of men, as well as to pray for them').[1] Pascal was to sharpen his wit against them in later years, but for the moment his urgent need was to help his friends find God by recognising the special nature of the heart's response when not dulled by meaningless activity or warped by self-interest. Although this would not have been of great interest to the pleasure-loving French society surrounding the Sun King, these were decades when emotions were under scrutiny, whether in the salons of the *grandes dames* or in the merciless writings of France's great playwrights – especially

---

1 Page 113.

Molière, whose portraits of megalomaniacs urged a curbing of irrational obsession, and Racine, who knew that this was not always possible and that tragic consequences seem inevitable on the human plane.

Pascal saw that there are advantages to these 'reasons that reason knows not of'; that, freed from the constraints of rational thought processes, the suppliant heart could be open to truth. Expanding the traditional division of mind from body, he posits a third part, which he called *l'ordre de la charité*, entered into by means of *l'esprit de finesse*, whose vehicle was the heart.

'Is it the Lover's heart you'd have us heed?
Its flowery sentiments, its passionate need?
And, granting these, are we to trust
Its declarations or its hidden lust?'

'No, more the scheming heart you'd have us see
Sheds reason's sense, its own integrity;
Persuades the soul which wants and needs God's grace
With vile agendas which that grace displace.'

'Yet, God is love, and human hearts can be
Channels of his grace, if they but bend the knee.'

(*Il faut plier les genoux du Cœur*)

HEADSTRONG HEART

Carmen's gypsy boy, my heart flings
Wide the shutters in the blinding
Sun, spurns doors, paths, signposts. Bounds
Headlong. Stubs toes, tears limbs, in his heading
For the headland. There, sun-blinded, spins round
(Tongue out, rude boy) to show my nervous self
Emblazoned on his front: 'The Heart Has Reasons.'
And there, just half a step behind, the crumbling edge
Crumbles. And the blind, headstrong boy trusting in . . .
(But faith and faithfulness are lost)
God knows what wings.

ON THE OCCASION OF MY NEPHEW'S WEDDING

The stirring of the heart
A source that bubbles deep below,
That gurgles like a fountain plays
Quite undisturbed by reason's ways.
Its power, reaching like a dart,
Issues from brighter, hidden depth;
Its deep-drawn purity apart
From channelled waterways of mind
Unlinked to reason's ways.
Until these channels start to block,
Unworkable through age.
Then tired or sick or overworked
You'll welcome reasoning from the heart.

5

MIRACLES – THE ONE HE DARES TO CLAIM; CONCUPISCENCE – THE SIN HE DARES TO NAME

B Y 1655 PORT-ROYAL WAS FEELING THE EFFECTS of the disapproval and suspicion of Jansenism that, promoted by the Jesuits, was increasing in the ranks of the Church. Pascal would have shared this discomfort, and welcomed all the more the apparently miraculous cure of his niece, Marguerite Périer. A relic which was kept and venerated at Port-Royal was believed to be a thorn from Jesus' crown of thorns. Through contact with it, it appeared that Marguerite was cured of a fistula on the eye. In his *Déposition sur le miracle de la Sainte Épine* (which can be read in the Lafuma complete works on page 672), Pascal gives testimony to the total cure. He was overjoyed by this miracle shown to his god-daughter. In his sister's biography she writes, 'His joy was so great that he was entirely absorbed by it, and as he never turned his mind to anything without a great deal of reflection, this miracle provided him with the opportunity for a number of very important reflections, concluding that there must be something above what we call nature.'[2]

As in our own age of scientific advance, seventeenth-century thinkers were both sceptical of and fascinated by the inexplicable, the miraculous. In *Pensée* 169, Pascal quotes St Augustine, who says he would not be Christian without the miracles, and devotes a whole section (Series XXII–XXIV) to their discussion.

---

2 Quoted from *Pascal's Pensées*, translated by Martin Turnell.

Miracle

The passing down of the holy
Into matter began
With the word made flesh.
From then, small distance
To the healing hands
And the hem of his garment.
After then, the institution of
Bread and wine, and after
Upon his head
The mocking crown,
The crown
Of which may be
This thorn.

Concluding, as his sister reports, that 'there must be something above nature', Pascal returned to that study of human nature. He had already pinpointed diversion, constant activity, as something which confuses and distracts from the spiritual. He now turned to something more deep-rooted, discovering – as have all the God-fearing of all ages and creeds – that the obstacles to spiritual growth lie in uncontrolled desire. These temptations to excess he names 'concupiscences' and defines them as the tendency to give greater weight to worldly values than to spiritual realities. That which stems from our in-built (animal) need to survive is the least pernicious, and recognition of this material need leads to caring leadership.

I

Concupiscence
The body's greed
Simple, straightforward, focused need
(Or need perceived,
And oft deceived
By fears of fallow years ahead)
To hoard our stocks of meat and bread;
Insure against the final dread
Of offspring who cannot be fed.

II

Cramming our mouths full of berries
Our pockets full of nuts,
We learn the first concupiscence
Of our humanity. It shuts
Doors on our soul's full growth,
But opens other ways to truth.
Thus, caring for the poor and needy
Stems from the days when we were greedy,
And bountiful ruling is nothing less
Than the pleasant extension of our success
Into highly publicised largesse.

More to be feared are the less evident passions:

CONCUPISCENCE OF THE MIND

Do not let cold ambition rule your mind
Or let the drive to dominate colour your thought.
To others' inspiration be not blind.
You need to know their work; have their support.

Concupiscence of the heart

One who surrenders to the heart's desire
And lets its passions be his aim,
Discovers that this love can tire,
And struggles to be free again.

Focusing on humanity's weakness, Pascal chooses to show the
inexhaustible depths of sin and depravity open to it, once it has forsaken
God. Looking beyond the medieval vision of heaven and hell, he sought
to help his contemporaries gain insight into the motivation behind their
behaviour. Starting, as any good psychologist must, with himself, he
helps his readers in their self-examination:

Intrepid Pascal, in an age
When tailored words and well-turned coats were all the rage,
To put under the microscope yourself.
Deprived of charm, prestige or wealth,
Disclosing shame, our shared disgrace.
The hidden secrets of our restless race.

Rotating mirrors, turn of phrase
Enable me to see
Unpalatable me.

6

THE WAGER

It is wiser to wager, and better to bet
For a God whose existence has not been disproved yet.
(my paraphrase)

THE EXISTENCE OR NON-EXISTENCE OF GOD could not allow for compromise. The agnostic, Pascal saw, must choose. He saw too just how difficult such a leap of faith could be. He could enter into blunt dialogue with Montaigne; as Krailsheimer observed: 'His reaction to Montaigne's flight to a hammock of ignorance and indolence was to rock it so vigorously that even bare ground seemed preferable.' For his friends at the gaming table, however, he offered something more positive, choosing to introduce the idea of religion by means of a reasonable betting proposition, which would make mathematical sense and offer a way of changing direction. Kreeft observes[1] that faith is not a wager but a relationship; however, it can begin with a wager, just as marriage can begin with a blind date.

As twentieth-century philosophers would say, we are 'embarqués'. If we are not straining in the right direction, we are drifting in the wrong one. (Indeed, Sartre would go further, to declare that humankind betrays its heritage, if not *engagé* according to truths perceived.) Philosophy in the seventeenth century was still occupied with attempts to prove the existence of God. Pascal did not offer a theological exposé or doctrinal study. His thoughts were not being put forward as cornerstones of a mental edifice that would define creation. What he offers are landmarks

1 BBC Radio 4, 'In Our Time', 19 September 2013.

from his own spiritual experience. He counts on his readers beginning the acquisition of faith by wanting it so much that they are prepared to make sacrifices. That is his aim in presenting the disappointments and frustrations we meet in purely human activity, but he also summons the anxiety we feel at the thought of missing out on a rich experience. *Pensée* 387 speaks for one truly more worried to find Christianity, which he had dismissed, to be true than to find his belief ill-founded.

DIALOGUE

'So, for your God you'd have me stake all that I love,
When his existence reason cannot prove?'
'You reason well. His Being being on a higher plane
Our arguments and proofs are all in vain.'
'So, with these equal odds I still should bet?'
'Indeed you must, and I would show you yet
With cold statistics that if you should lose
You lose no more at death than if you wore a pauper's shoes,
But, if you win, you win infinity
And heaven's joys for all eternity.'
'And if the angel choirs have no appeal
While earth has still sweet joys that I would steal?'
'He who created earth must know its pleasure.
Trust then the heavenly measure.'

* * *

Not for me?
I'm not a gambling girl.
Say no to raffles,
No friend of Lady Luck.
Plough my own furrow
With the sweat of my brow;
'No pain, no gain', I reason
When the going gets tough.
'All my own work',
When it goes well enough.
'Thanks. Got my life sorted'
(To Pascal at my shoulder).
'And the afterlife?'
As he places a betting board
Over my seeded furrows,
And a hand of compassion
Over my furrowed, anxious brow.
'Not in the ill-lit labyrinth of the mind,'
(Though his is crystal clear and bright as day)
'But choose within the safer, sheltered soul.'

7

'THE SOLE CAUSE OF MAN'S UNHAPPINESS IS THAT HE IS UNABLE TO SIT QUIETLY IN HIS ROOM'

'THE BEST PHILOSOPHY', Pascal wrote, 'is to make fun of philosophy.' Neither happiness nor truth can be reached by dashing round after them. From his own experience, he recommended taking time to seek in solitude, pointing out repeatedly that endless distraction and meaningless activity deprive us of an intimate experience of our own being and of the ground of that being.

In the end, wisdom dictates a personal remedy for the ills of society. For the individual finding his spiritual aspirations impeded by the demands and concerns of a busy world that is engaged only with the temporal, Pascal's recommendation is to cultivate quiet receptivity. He would have known how difficult this is even for the Religious.

It is told that a novice, feeling restless in his soul, sought out an older monk, who advised him to return to his cell and pray. Unsatisfied with this advice, he sought out another member of the older community. This monk sensed that the novice had come in order to find distraction. 'Do not attempt to pray now,' he advised, 'but you must return to your cell.'

Give me my bow of burning gold
Like good St George you'll find me brave and bold
I'll slay the dragon, bear and serpent.

Do not, I beg, constrain me in my cell
Where insubstantial ghouls and spirits dwell.
Such soulful struggle's not at all my penchant.

Perhaps Pascal's 'room' is a compartment of the soul where stillness is to be found in which to discover our intended purpose in the world.

So, in the château of my soul,
Which room should I select to place my chair?
To shun distraction, is the dungeon where
I'll find the calm to set my soul at rest?
No, there I know to be a viper's nest
Of basest thoughts and selfishness repressed.
Should I in such miasma place
My being thirsting for Thy grace?
Is not the gallery more fit
A context where to choose to sit
And see Thy splendour mirrored on the walls?
But here, admit, self-satisfaction calls
And smug delight in all the praise I've won
Since self-promotion's first begun.
I'll choose instead to mount the stair,
And in the turret place my chair.
Then see, outside the castle gates – and make my care –
A hungry world in need of more than food.
And for its sake, I'll glean the dancing air
And find my little room suffused with gratitude.

8

THE LAST YEARS

THE QUIET, RATHER PRIVATE MAN who, in the eyes of Steinmann and Eastwood, could be thought of as a mystic, who had willingly buried the fame he had acquired as prodigy and eminent scientist to give himself to God with greater devotion, was soon to find himself in the public gaze again.

In 1656, in spite of ill health, he undertook the defence of Jansenism against the accusations of the Jesuits by publishing eighteen anonymous letters, ostensibly to a friend in the provinces. In these he pointed out the lax morality which resulted from the accommodating ethics prevalent among certain Jesuits at that time. This brought into relief, for the Church and the individual, the value of the stricter behavioural code of the Jansenists.

The letters do not engage in theological or doctrinal issues. Pascal never subscribed to the element of exclusivity detectable in some strands of Jansenism, but they were merciless in their depiction of what has been termed 'casuistry' (over-complex or plausible-seeming but false arguments). As literature, they have been admired through the ages for their acute observation and wit, and again one may see why he was becoming unpopular in some quarters while welcomed in others.

If painful guilt upon your conscience sits,
Best make your confession to the Jesuits.
They will convince you if you have the time
That your most heinous sin is not really a crime;
That if you consider it in the right light,
It is perfectly natural and 'really all right'.
So wrote Pascal with the Jansenist persuasion
That grace cannot operate with such evasion.
Over Jesuit casuistry the Church drew a veil:
Put Pascal and his letters outside the pale.
This view may well stay with the Church to this day:
'But wasn't Pascal Protestant?' his fellow Catholics say.

His last years were marked by physical discomfort and painful decline. After his sister Jacqueline's death in 1661, he waited for his own death, and asked to be transferred to the hospital for incurables. He had known that he was severely ill from the beginning of February 1662 and in spite of – or perhaps because of – the medical services offered to him by the most reputable physicians, including the queen's own doctor, his condition grew steadily worse.

The seventeenth century, for all its growing atheism and secular pursuits, was marked by a number of men showing exceptional charity. Pierre de Bérulle combined the virtues of the *honnête homme* with piety, and Francis de Sales and Vincent de Paul found their total vocation in helping the poor and sick. 'For the monastery,' wrote the former 'use the houses of the poor; for the cloister, the streets.' Pascal should be included in their number. The testimony of his surviving sister, Gilberte Périer, records how he became more and more concerned for the poor who were deprived of the attention he was being given, and asked that one of the poor of the parish be brought in to be with him, to benefit from all the care he received. He deeply regretted that he had not given more time to the needs of the poor throughout his life. Perhaps he felt that in his own suffering he could appreciate something of their deprivation, and understand why Christ loved those who boasted of nothing – why

He commended an unimpeded life. One of Pascal's last projects was an omnibus, a *cinq sous*, a means of public transport for those who could not afford a carriage.

On 19 August 1662 Pascal suffered a brain haemorrhage and died, only ten months after the death of his sister. Unlike so many of his contemporaries, he had not ignored the inevitability and reality of death. In words which have a Shakespearean ring, he observed: 'The last act is bloody, however fine the rest of the play.' We know that his last hours were neither pain free nor dignified, but it would seem that his very acceptance of death enabled him to meet it with composure. He had written – with one of those images that haunt us down the centuries – that we are like men chained together, obliged to watch as one after another is killed, knowing that our turn must come. But hope had not deserted him.

The goal of saints and hermits,
Stripped and shorn
Of wealth and health
And all the cushioned shell
We see the world provide.
They see the pearl inside,
Rejoice that they are poor
And can perceive the door
Through which true joys reside.

As pain which tears the body, sears the soul,
Will stultify the mind and check its course,
What wonder, then, that you in constant pain
Could think so clearly, with such power as yours.
What wonder to perceive your mental might,
While yet your mind was locked in tortured shell.
Your spirit, agile as a bird in flight,
Sought which of all your thoughts your pen should tell.

9

THE *PENSÉES*, SKETCHES FOR AN APOLOGIA

THE REPUTATION PASCAL ENJOYED at his death was enormous. Hailed as a genius in the scientific arena, he was also revered as a man of letters; but his thoughts, the *Pensées* for which he is known today, were not in general circulation at that time. They were found after his death by his nephew, Étienne Périer. They were mostly on scraps of paper threaded together into bundles (*les liasses*); these are known as the *Papiers classés*. Others were left randomly. All were handed over to Port-Royal, who arranged, classified and perhaps edited according to their knowledge of Pascal and their own lights. This edition was brought out in 1670.

There followed many attempts at classifying and ordering. The autograph copy was not rediscovered until early in the twentieth century, when Léon Brunschvicg brought out an edition which seemed faithful to the original. The Lafuma edition of 1963, which is represented here in Krailsheimer's translation, offered a different classification – a different ordering of the *Pensées*. This is the most readily available English version, which is why I follow it here. The most recent edition in English of which I am aware is Roger Ariew's; he bases his translation on the edition brought out by Philippe Sellier in 1976. His classification is based on what is referred to as copy B. Ariew considers this to be the most faithful manuscript. All the latest French editions follow Sellier's classification.

As a seventeenth-century writer, Pascal did not feel the need to be original in terms of material. 'It is the same tennis ball that is used,' he writes, 'but the players deal with it in different ways.' What was important to him was the presentation, to give his thoughts their maximum impact, so as to arrest and persuade. It is clear that he gave much consideration to the order they should be given.

Section II, 'Commencement', is placed at the start of Brunschvicg's classification and, as Kreeft points out, its focus is death. The first of the *Papiers classés*, however, is in the bipartite form he intends to give his Apologia. A simple enough formula:

> A. Wretchedness of Man without God;
> B. Happiness of Man with God.

We see him linking this with his other two-part distinction: the impossibility of finding God with *l'esprit de géométrie* – the tools of reason and logic; and the more appropriate means offered by *l'esprit de finesse*. The human condition provides both forms of mental activity, just as it is composed of natural (animal) instincts and supernatural aspirations. It is paradoxical – a situation, Pascal writes, which results from the dual nature of God Incarnate, who destroyed death by dying. Dorothy Eastwood in *The Revival of Pascal* describes Pascal's style as centripetal, the concurrence of ideas expressed in various guises. It is also characterised by paradox, or more correctly antinomy, in which contrary ideas are presented and balanced against one another. (One might even describe this, which appeals as much to the ear as the mind, as antiphony.) The power and poetry of his style have had many admirers. Jean Steinmann refers to the *Pensées* as 'a great poem, which swarms with religious and philosophical ideas, clothed like characters in medieval allegories'.

Paradox is Pascal's favoured stylistic tool. *Pensées* 578 and 675 commend unaffected expression, but he knows his art and in 91 and 691 he speaks of means of verbal persuasion. The method referred to above is used notably to present opposing theological or philosophical standpoints, with the purpose of seeing them cancel one another out, so as to leave room for a third, more acceptable proposal. One might instance the contention that to admit only reason as a means of reaching truth is as foolish as to exclude it altogether from the process of enquiry. Antithesis is present throughout. Martin Turnell lists: head in opposition to heart; faith to reason; religion and the religious; infinitely great and infinitely small; philosophy and philosophers; church and churches; and, principally, man's greatness and his wretchedness.

Pascal's style may be said to echo his message: 'Know, Man, that you are paradox.' The section 'Contrariétés' provides terse, succinct reminders of the contradictions encountered in humankind, and in common chosen lifestyles. It is interesting to note that he gives his imagination freer rein when writing of his faith, inviting the reader to do likewise whenever he ends with 'etc.' Pascal always has his reader in mind. As Steinmann observes, not wishing to be thought a philosopher or a theologian, he 'presents a solace to the honest doubter and a scandal to the aggressive unbeliever'.

CONTRARIWISE

I ventured to consult a tree to find the wind's direction
But buffeted and tossed was he, and branches blown in
    contradiction.
How like myself I had to see
This sorry, gnarled and tortured tree.

That hawthorn on a windy ridge I wish I could implore
To cast his seed on kindlier plain, so that his trunk, like
    constant thought,
Could firm through storms remain.
But tireless winds have set his fate,
And I will weep no more.

Et Cetera
With which your work is peppered.
In another age, you might have said:
Conversationally,
'Well, you know what I mean,'
And latterly, 'And all that stuff'.
Instead this portal to your own vast thinking,
Reaching to the borders of things.
This and all that is.
And so forth . . .
World without end,
Without limit.

10

TWO INFINITIES

THE DEVELOPMENT OF THE TELESCOPE was accompanied, in Pascal's lifetime, by that of the microscope. The world which was just coming to terms with the implications of the vast universe opened up by Galileo's discoveries was also confronted by a new awareness of the complexity of matter.

Like the Greeks, Descartes maintained that the universe was infinitely large because the imagination can stretch beyond the idea of space indefinitely extended, but he believed the atom to be indivisible. Pascal, who, in the words of Steinmann, 'made infinity his vocation' after his conversion, saw the possibility of the infinitely vast universe being matched by infinitely divisible particles within matter. These two infinities, which he greeted with wonder and awe, provided much of the inspiration of the *Pensées*. He saw wider implications. He was concerned to show humankind perched between the two: very small in comparison with the vast universe; very big in comparison with what the microscope could reveal.

In morality, too, Pascal speaks of two infinities: our infinite capacity to know God offset by an infinite capacity for sin, which could place us at an infinite distance from God, were it not for his grace. There were many in the seventeenth century, that time of multi-faceted religious fervour, who aspired to union with the divine through different forms of piety and asceticism. Pascal's advice – that we strive to know ourselves for what we are – implies a plumbing of the depths of our unpalatable nature; a truthful and meticulous examination of motives and selfish tendencies so as to provide space in which grace might operate.

Cupping its hand in arrogance,
Thinking to contain all the microscope could reveal,
The seventeenth century marvelled only upwards
At the infinity of galaxies,
A universe fit for man's equations;
Infinity to match his aspirations.
Prising open the cupped hand,
New mathematics showed infinity burrowing inwards,
Opening out space between fractions,
Increasing the declining potential
Of men bereft of God's guidance.

Les deux infinis

I would go for stargazing
Out of preference;
For scaling dizzy heights,
Knowing there to be a taller peak beyond.
I would opt for aching limbs,
Because the crowd below would cheer;
Would welcome thirst and deprivation,
If I can win a hero's crown.

But they are, in my heart I know,
Real heroes who go down below;
Who delve through layers of pretence,
(Calling a spade a spade,
Leaving no crack disguised)
Into that cleft gouged out by sin's monotony,
Shaft without end or finality,
Reason for our mortality.

But then, the Saviour who knew these realms in death,
Stretches down a hand to land them safe.

II

POISED

Pascal's unique view of humanity poised between two infinities obviously has a resemblance to the medieval concept of heaven and hell. But times were changing and new insights into human behaviour revealed that concept as an oversimplification of the human condition, recognising that there is paradox in human nature itself: creative, yet destructive too; subscribing to preordained patterns, yet wired for self-preservation at all costs; programmed for renewal, yet forever uncertain as to the way to achieve this, because the Creator is invisible to mortal eyes. In contrast to these opposing forces, Pascal encourages the soul to believe that by truly seeking Christ, it will behold him as the one promise of ultimate synthesis in a union in space and time.

Together with the astronomical discoveries opened up by the telescope, seventeenth-century thought benefited from exploration of a more earthbound kind. As new territories were discovered, the nature of the human species was given a wider interpretation. Montaigne contrasted the primitive tribes in America with the Europeans who would aim to civilise them, finding more natural virtue in the former. This commonly idealised picture of the noble savage is not to be found in Pascal. In entreating his readers to know themselves, he is asking for recognition of shared human nature, characterised by 'inconstancy, boredom, anxiety' (*Pensée* 24). At the same time there is an aspiration for something finer: 'We are equally incapable of knowing and of a desire not to know' (*Pensée* 75).

Kreeft[1] applies this placing of humankind in the universe, where there has to be a balancing of aspiration against limitation, to our modern age of moral relativism, where awareness of the two extremes persuades us to question our standpoint.

Poised
As a bird might be for powerful flight
(Or our smart selves for flight mechanically engineered
When cleverness exceeded caution);
Or else the well-trained body on the edge,
Poised over chlorine-blue, or green – pebble reflecting,
Trusting weight-sustaining waters for a graceful dive.
It is for us to learn the balancing of our weight;
To keep from plummeting deep,
Where weighty nature bears its sons away;
Fells trees to give the sapling space;
And watches sparrows fall to feed the hawk.

A different danger comes with pride
That tells the soul to rise above
Where weightless angels breathe an air
Too rarefied for human lungs.
Ensuing madness then can cause a jump
Where nothing balances the downward trend,
Where weight grown weightier from human dread,
Stifles creative thought
And cuts the senses dead.

Too much knowledge leads to pride,
Too little to despair.
What wisdom led you, gracious God,
To place us in a limited abode
And meet us there.

---

1 Pages 163–6.

I 2

THE ABYSS

Le silence éternel de ces espaces infinies m'effraie.
(The eternal silence of these infinite spaces fills me with fear.)

IN THE SEVENTEENTH CENTURY, INFINITY REPRESENTED THE VOID.
It was seen as what occurred at the extremity of the universe, the abyss
from which we come and into which we seem bound to return.
The possible existence of vacuum presented a problem for theology. It
seemed unthinkable that God's creation, teeming with life, which he had
pronounced good, could contain absence of being. One could not allow
'nothing' into the picture without questioning his omnipotence. Pascal,
as mathematician, knew the existence of nothing was fundamental, and
that our perception of creation must get adjusted to allow for it.

As has been seen, the pivotal moment in Pascal's life, the determinant
for his life's work, occurred on 23 November 1654. In gratitude for
this confirmation of his own faith, he longed for his friends to achieve
recognition of the claims of Christ for themselves, and he addressed
those who genuinely wished to find what he had found. The biggest
obstacle to the seeker is the awesome nature of the search, the abject fear
which can accompany confrontation with the void, the abyss, the region
beyond our knowledge.

Pascal does not sneer at those who experience a sort of terrified
paralysis at the thought of this. He too has stood at the brink of these
unfathomable realities, and felt their inexorable power. What he does
condemn is the way so many well-meaning, cultured *honnêtes hommes*
aimed to stifle this and other unpleasant realities by means of constant

activity. Section VII of the *Pensées* is called 'Diversion', and is devoted to the investigation of this evasive behaviour. 'Being unable to cure death, wretchedness, ignorance, men have decided , in order to be happy, not to think about such things . . . That is why they are so fond of hustle and bustle.' However, even this they get wrong, finding that when they achieve what they thought would make them happy, they are thrown back into a boredom such that could poison the whole mind.

Two centuries before Baudelaire, but in the tradition of those mystics who experienced accidie – a kind of spiritual apathy – Pascal identified ennui as the scourge of the human soul. The truly great walk through this desert in the dark night of the soul, and experience our vertiginous perch mid-way between all and nothing; the rest of us, Pascal observes, fill our days with frantic, often worthless activity, so as not to know this.[1]

In the section entitled 'Contrariétés' (*Pensées* 119–131), Pascal stands alongside the sceptics, or, more correctly, the Pyrrhonists, in admitting that nothing can be known for sure this side of the grave. The next section, however, is called 'Transition from Knowledge of Man to Knowledge of God', and concludes with 'Two considerations to complete the proof of our weakness'. The first, introducing the image of the 'thinking reed', asserts that all our dignity consists in thought, advising that we 'think well'. The second proof of our weakness sounds like a *cri de cœur*, and has often been taken as an expression, a confession of the writer's own fears. 'The eternal silence of these infinite spaces fills me with fear.' From the context, however, it is clear that Pascal is still displaying the weakness, the wretchedness he sees in the human condition when dissociated from God. The *Pensée* following reads 'Be comforted' and suggests that confidence can be regained by re-introducing God into the picture.

---

1 Kreeft observes (page 187) that until the seventeenth century people were not bored. The ancients had no word for it. 'Accidie', a concept similar to 'boredom', was seen as indifference to our eternal destiny. (It is defined in the *OED* as applying to the mental prostration of recluses, sometimes used synonymously for 'sloth'; 'ennui' is defined as 'a feeling of mental weariness and dissatisfaction, produced by want of occupation or interest in present surroundings'.

Ennui

Stepping stones. Dates in my diary.
Far from apologetic, I label these importantly,
Polish them daily. Unaware
That the polished surface
Offers a mirror to my vanity;
To their own inanity.
Most emphatically
I do not turn them over,
For fear of what may crawl from beneath
To blight my achievement;
What blanched weed would spread
To impoverish my soul's soil.
My soul! Master Pascal, do I not blush to recall
The fair meadow given for its cultivation?
Now littered and spare,
For all I do is to avoid
The void.

II

With restless inertia, pallid effulgence,
Ennui casts its net,
Entrapping thoughts, projects, dreams
Which squirm like half-dead fish,
Knowing they cannot now avoid
The void.

LE SILENCE ÉTERNEL DE CES ESPACES INFINIES M'EFFRAIE

Your interlocutor's words, of course.
Not yours, man of science
At home with Creation;
With figures and distances.
Not you, poet of the soul;
Explorer of the unknown;
Cartographer of profundities.
Not you, fervent God-fearer,
Who knew your frail body
(Tossed by mortal tides)
Would land you in this realm
Sooner than later,
In this blessed realm
Of unblemished stillness.

II

Forever silence in forever space.
A chill wind skirts the corners of your soul?
A chasm shudders open in the mind?
Yet, 'Silence I love,' I'll say,
'Precious oasis in a noisy world,'
'Transparent moment in my life's opacity.'
(The lush, rich thing I'm thinking of on earth,
Studded with munching cows or chirping birds
Or happy laughs in children's games.)
Now, though, consider distance distancing
In thin, consumptive silence, petering out into everything . . .
Into nothing, with the question still unanswered . . .
'Was it the rectitude of arithmetic that held you as you peered,
Held you firm and fearless?
Or did you detect that in that unfathomable nadir
Dwells the substance of the hidden God?' [2]

---

2 The hidden God, *Deus absconditus*. That God is hidden was a much-voiced objection among Pascal's fellow thinkers. 'How much more readily we would believe in him, if we had evidence of his existence.' Pascal understands this problem, and returns to it throughout his writing. In the fourth letter to the brother and sister De Roannez (Lafuma, page 267), he states that we produce the veil ourselves by the way we live, but he considers also that our very human state, midway between the infinitely great and the infinitely small, necessitates that we are shown only partially. Not suited to extreme heat or extreme cold, we must accept a happy medium in all things. This he explores in a number of *Pensées*: in 57, that it is equally foolish to exclude reason and to admit nothing else, and in the cryptic and jocular 38:'Too much wine . . . too little wine.'

13

ANGEL OR BEAST?

THE PORTRAYAL OF HUMANITY, placed midway between all and nothing, big in comparison with the infinitely small, small in the light of the universe, runs as a thread throughout the *Pensées*. The paradoxical nature of humanity itself, which finds its loftiest aspirations hampered by our bodily limitations and material impulses, Pascal declares to be explained by our being neither angel nor beast, although we have elements of both (*Pensée* 678). This might suggest the dualistic philosophy which characterised the Middle Ages, separating mind and body into irreconcilable camps. Pascal did indeed consider that mind and body operate on two different planes; more, that the selfish tendencies which result from our animal nature must be restrained if we are to make spiritual progress. What distinguishes his thought, however, is that he posited a third order of operation. This he called charity, which, received as grace, could regulate the action of both mind and body. *Le moi est haïssable* (the self is hateful), that stark advice he offers to his friend Damien Mitton, is not simply an exhortation to unselfishness, but a reassurance that, with the help of faith, one can deny all that comes with our inbuilt animal competitiveness.

Pensée 121 provides a caution not just to those who see humanity only as bestial, but also to those who deny the body its own role. The Incarnation is a reminder that grace was and is transmitted to us through the flesh. Kreeft[1] writes of 'the two disastrous errors of animalism and angelism, both of which deprive us of our true identity', going on to suggest that it is not so much our animal selves that go astray: 'Roses cannot be un-rosy . . . but humans can be inhuman.'

---

1 Page 55.

Prayer in response to Pascal's exhortation

Angelic aspirations? Wretched beast!
Pascal, you'd have us scrutinise our human state,
And, so our spirit's surge can be increased,
Look out the animal within which we must hate.
And yet, cranes fly with unwarped instinct south
And swans unconsciously are truly Swan.
Since we can never wholly spirit be
While part of earth's creation,
Help us our truest self to see
And shelter it from harmful deviation.

14

MAN IS A REED,
BUT A THINKING REED

As we have seen, Pascal recognised the sense of vertigo, of insecurity which arose from awareness of the abyss over which human life is straddled. 'What is Man in the infinite?' he voices in *Pensée* 113. 'Man is equally incapable of seeing the nothingness from which he emerges and the infinite in which he is engulfed.' We cannot dismiss the astonishing realities of our situation, but nor can we underestimate the worth of thought. (*Pensée* 759: 'Thought constitutes Man's greatness'.)

In an age when Protestant theology encouraged believers to stand with self-assurance in the presence of their saviour, with whom they could enjoy direct communication, and when, with the Renaissance, scientists and philosophers felt confident that in time they could understand and master the world and the whole of creation, Pascal's representation of humanity would have startled, if not shocked. That man stands weak and spineless in the face of nature, whose slightest vicissitudes could destroy him, is recognised today, but would have seemed unduly pessimistic in the aristocratic circles of seventeenth-century France.

Pascal presents the other side of the coin, however, by highlighting our crowning glory: thought – through which we are more powerful than anything the universe can present. 'It is not in space that I must find my dignity, but in the ordering of my thought,' he writes in *Pensée* 113. 'It will do me no good to own land. Through space, the universe grasps me, and swallows me up like a speck; through thought I grasp it.' And again in *Pensée* 200: 'Even if the universe were to crush him, man would be nobler than his slayer, because he knows he is dying and the advantage the universe has over him. The universe knows none of this.'

Pascal recognised that our suffering results from our having the power of thought. Animals do not experience spiritual malaise. Wretchedness is part of our human condition. Thought is given to help us opt for right. 'Let us then strive to think well. That is the basis of morality.'

Roseau pensant

Unlovely image!
Whether the sappy frame was topped with sculpted head
(Renaissance marble made magnificent)
Or else, as now, rhomboid severity
(For electronic thoughts).
Unlovely image, harsh Pascal!
(There was, of course, a brief interval:
Romantic sentiment favoured the fragile reed;
Man subject to nature's whims, tossed by tides,
Manfully striding on.)
Now that man's thought foresees
That reedy beds could drown
Or shrivel in the too hot sun,
His thought must know his fate;
Its need to prevent the funereal date
When it could be too late.

15

'YOU WOULD NOT SEEK ME, IF YOU HAD NOT ALREADY FOUND ME'

THE TEXT OF THE *PENSÉES* abounds with commendation for the honest seeker. Following St Augustine, Pascal writes in *Pensée* 631 'It is good to be tired and weary from fruitlessly seeking the true good, so that one can stretch out one's arms to the Redeemer.' He does not wish to leave us at rest, because he knows that a restless heart is the second best thing to finding the way. Again with Augustine, he speaks of the soul's repose once it has found what (whom) it seeks.

'Agnosticism is the only true philosophical stand,' he maintains in 691. 'If it is concrete proof you are after, you will not find it in this world where all is uncertain.' He finds much to admire in Montaigne, but criticises those among his followers who see in his philosophy a 'soft pillow of ignorance' to justify apathy and inertia. More fiercely, in *Pensée* 886, he describes the sceptic as obstinate; he has clearly had some unproductive exchanges. His most telling comment is in *Pensée* 405: 'I can only approve of those who seek with groaning [*en gémissant*].'

Pascal wrote of the limitations of deism and the less Christocentric forms of Protestantism, which he considered as far removed from Christianity as atheism, in that they do not respond to the summons of the Gospel. With Rousseau and the nineteenth-century Romantics, nature was seen as the place in which to experience the divine. Two centuries earlier, deism had followed a similar a-religious path. Pascal, too, experienced wonder and delight in the created world, but saw that to lose the sense of a personal relationship with the Trinity could result in the cold ritual which so alienated his friends.

Roger Ariew calls *Pensées* 427–431 (Series III in Lafuma and Krailsheimer) 'A letter to further the search for God'. Pascal allows the seeker to give full expression to doubts and anxieties, but also asks for a critical look at the way life is lived by so many: 'Those who live without a thought for the end of life … as if they could annihilate eternity by keeping their minds off it.' He then gives voice to one of a more appropriate disposition: 'My whole heart strains to know what the true good is so as to pursue it.' Indeed, as Pascal so often repeated, it is the heart which is best suited to this quest, and fervent desire for truth which provides the best motivation.

Pensées 919–949 – a section in the non-classified *Pensées* entitled 'Mystère de Jésus' – strike a more personal note than we find in the classified numbers. They may be seen as a dialogue between the saviour and the soul. In 929 we find the well-known sentence quoted in the chapter title. It reassures all the more with the sentence which follows: 'Do not be troubled.' It calls for a very personal response.

> Oh, yes, we have found You
> In the mind's marvelling at the majesty of mountains;
> The eyes ecstatic scanning of distant plains.
> In the heart's trembling at a thrush's note,
> Dilating with an early celandine.
> What we now seek is
> A long-term lodging
> In that reservoir of longing,
> Shaped, Augustine wrote,
> Fashioned and reserved
> For Your own self
> Alone.

16

'ACT AS IF YOU BELIEVED'

'THE HEART HAS ITS REASONS THAT REASON KNOWS NOT OF.' This most famous quotation runs as a thread throughout the intended Apologia, as the secret from which an answer can be found to the pervasive question: 'How can we know God?' Dismissing the idea that he can be reached through philosophy, Pascal recognises the value of intuition and the instinctive response of the heart. *Dieu sensible au cœur* (God known [only] to the heart).

If Descartes can be thought of as philosopher of the mind, Pascal must be seen as philosopher of the heart. In his scrutiny of human behaviour, he recognised that emotion and instinct control our actions as much as reason and logic; that unthinking, mechanical reactions can be sounder than calculated ones, because the heart is given full rein. Pascal knew that the heart has its reasons.

The logic presented in the Pascal's wager, if it persuades through reason, could still suggest a worrying leap of faith. It was not Pascal's way to leave his readers in the cold of indecision. Throughout the *Pensées* he offers the reassurance that God's way is one of love. More than this, ever practical, he suggests that the possible convert work with a trial period, acting as if (*comme si*) he or she believed. It is significant that he recommends practices which are least defensible from a rational point of view: having masses said for the dead, taking holy water. He could have suggested visiting the sick or giving to the poor, but the disciple of Montaigne would have argued that this was just good humanism.

Pascal recognised the value of subduing rational argument for a period so as to develop mechanical habits which would later be seen as natural expressions of a faith accepted by the mind as well as by the heart. This adopting of habitual behaviour he recommended for letting a wholesome instinct take over when the mind is troubled. 'Your soul is an area of repose,' he declares, 'so act as if the matter is resolved in favour of belief.'

COMME SI

If I were to act as though I believed, I might
Read the Bible every day,
Or go on retreats
(Or maybe wear a cross at work
And risk being dismissed),
Tell my hostess I don't eat meat on Fridays
(And risk being a difficult guest),
Risk being thought a 'pi' do-gooder,
Hypocrite even.
But if the 'if' should crumble away
With glory cascading down the scree of scepticism;
If risks become adventure,
And doubts mere academic hypotheses;
Fear and anxiety cooled in the flow of
Truth streaming into eternity . . .

17

CONCUPISCENCE UNCONTROLLED PROVES AN OBSTACLE UNTOLD

Pascal names as 'concupiscence' any tendency which gives greater weight to worldly values than to spiritual realities, and recognises that it dogs those who seek after truth. He agrees with Montaigne that thinkers are likely to be guilty of intellectual pride. In fact he goes further, saying that arrogance puts even the finest minds 'behind bars'. In consequence, they are unable to reach out to God or to their colleagues. Human nature may be defined by 'inconstancy, anxiety, boredom', but those who have received the gift of creative thought should know how to regulate their attitude.

As a creative scientist and thinker, Pascal was well aware of the desire to be first in the field of discovery and acclaim, but he cautions that to give full rein to the arrogance that comes with creativity is harmful to the very work it promotes. Keith Devlin's recent documentation of the correspondence between Fermat and Pascal in *The Unfinished Game* provides evidence of the courtesy and generosity of spirit shared between these two great mathematicians.

TWIN TEMPTATIONS TO PRIDE AND CONCUPISCENCE

Theories incubated in well-padded minds
Emerge on jaunty legs to take
Shy shelter in their youth.
But when the antlers start to grow,
They long to lock in enmity,
Trumpet success, trample opponents' pride.
Such self-assertion does not serve the cause
Of science or theology.
'That which you see please show to me;
That which I do is yours to know.'

II

Ideas conceived in well-nourished brains
Stride out from incubation.
Fierce to assert themselves,
They seek a craggy top
From which they'll leap astride the foothills
Of debate, trampling all sapling views,
Whether in accord or not.
Then, should opposition rear in view,
They sharpen arrows tipped with wit
Or scorn, summon battalions.
Such competition must be fought.
If not, you miss the precious contribution
Of others' thought.

18

'WE WOULD NOT SEEK TRUTH
IF WE DID NOT LOVE IT'

'THE MOST BORING AND UNPRODUCTIVE QUESTION one can ask of religion', Alain de Botton states as his first sentence in *Religion for Atheists*, 'is whether or not it is true.' It would seem that Pascal likewise wasted little time arguing for or against the existence of God, preferring to show how ideally suited Christianity is to meeting the needs of humanity. He sees truth as too glorious to be squabbled over in words, emphasising again and again that it is to be perceived by the heart rather than by reason, with *l'esprit de finesse* rather than *l'esprit de géométrie*. In general he finds it more advantageous to display the errors of falsities masquerading as truths, so as to wipe the slate clean for true revelation, which he believes to be open to all who truly seek it.

The poem below was written at a time when the phrase it uses was
frequently heard in various media.

Recognising that 'nothing could be further from the truth,'
can we be hopeful?
Blind alleys – we are coming to know them;
To recognise the allure of mirages,
Temptations of Sirens,
And how to resist them.
Society is gradually getting real:
Tabloid tale-mongering is brought to task;
What celebrity says is no more held as 'gospel'.
Truth, still seeping out (with repentance and forgiveness
And from the mouths of babes and sucklings),
Trumps pompous pronouncements;
Is still gleaned from pulpit or platform
When one winnows out the chaff.
For truth took on human form
And spoke in human tongue
And does, though technology lays claim to fact
And science seeks out all that is
(But not what can be).
Facebook knows no humility
And hidden truths are not worth studying,
It seems. These come in startling blast,
'Shook foil' when all seems lost.

Hunting truth

Trumpets gold and clarion red
Summon battalions to your aid,
Proclaiming glory, strength and power.
If we would find the pure, the true,
We yet might look into a pond,
Or down into a flower.
And if not finding still
Might look again, again.

19

THE SEARCH FOR TRUTH AS A SOCIAL ISSUE

PASCAL WANTS HIS READERS to be able to 'sit quietly in a room', to sit back now and then and take stock, face up to realities about themselves and their position in creation by shunning distraction and meaningless activity. However, this should not suggest that he led some sort of detached, contemplative existence and was not engaged with the world and its needs. The journal kept by his sister Gilberte Périer shows a very different picture. His work in science and mathematics continued throughout his life (see, for example, *The History of Roulette* and *Of the Geometrical Spirit*, both written in 1658).

Religion, he maintained, was for living a better life; right thinking should enable us to take our rightful place in society. A purely personal faith would not conform to Christian teaching or help in times of crisis. It is only modern philosophy that has ceased to concern itself with putting the world to rights, in offering blueprints for society and remedies for its ills. The ancients saw this as the true goal of their calling to philosophical enquiry and, with the possible exception of Descartes, social involvement marked French philosophy in the decades following the Renaissance. That society got things wrong, that institutions failed, that the great and the good turned out to be neither were cause for questioning the status quo then as now. Philosophy was in no way at a standstill at that time and there was general recognition that human nature needed to be understood for the creation of good government.

In Section IX of the *Pensées*, entitled 'Philosophers', Pascal criticises the Stoics' misguided optimism, which suggests that we can have total control of our own actions. He recognises no less the arrogance of those who claim to be acting under God's personal guidance, and wreak havoc. As we have seen, he has more time for Montaigne, in whom he finds intellectual integrity. He criticises him harshly for not taking into account the immortality of the soul, but shares his respect for the simple faith of ordinary people.

Given our limited understanding and powers, moral values and an ethical framework can only be constructed in the light of what humanity might be. The Gospel, Pascal reminds us, puts love for neighbour second only to love for God.

> The seagull finds the highest rock;
> The blackbird sings from tallest tree.
> The nettle strives to top the dock.
> Nature in height seeks its supremacy.
> Yet, roots and moles most clearly show
> Burgeoning of power and darkest threats
> Are fashioned, worked on, down below.
> So, wider human hearts must grow
> Embracing others' struggles, come to know
> That that for which all nature strives
> Is needed to support more lives.

Collapse in my age or yours?

Caught on too steep proclivity
(To control the lurching
Zigzag between the tawdry hoardings),
Society's inevitable stumbling
May make the honest blush.
Those who would rush
To rescue and console
Flinch from the naked vision
Of sprawling imbecility,
Weighed down with acquisition.

What suitor can be found
To mate and match with such a fate?
You'd have Stoic and agnostic
File past and offer diagnostic.
But would reach for the template
(Hot from your night of fire)
And, seeing none to helpfully berate
Or cure, you set this stencil
On the wretch, and see the perfect fit.
Cinderella's slipper is our native faith.

20

IMAGINATION

WHAT ARE WE TO MAKE OF PASCAL'S DISTRUST of imagination, which he dubs *maîtresse d'erreur et de fausseté* – mistress of error and falsity? This facility, so dear to poets of later centuries, he sees, perhaps, more as the tendency to paint ourselves or others in fine colours and to be taken in by the masks the world presents. It feeds our preoccupations and 'enlarges the present by our thinking continually about it'. 'We are', he observes in *Pensée* 551, 'so caught up in the business of our earthly life and what we imagine would enhance it that these thoughts swamp the concerns we ought to have about eternity, to which we rarely give any thought at all.'

Like Montaigne, Pascal observes the extent to which society is influenced by the trappings of power and authority, giving some approval to this visual recognition of office in the robes worn by dignitaries of Church and State, while declaring that we are all the same beneath the surface. Imagination, then, can be seen as a haughty power: enemy of common reason, establishing in man a 'second nature' which suspends the evidence of the senses. However, Pascal does in that same *Pensée* (8), refer to it as 'supreme', 'the source of beauty, justice and happiness'. It may be a component of his prized *esprit de finesse*, precisely because it can overtake reason, and could be considered an essential tool in the search for truth. Pascal applauds all who seek truth, provided that when they find it, they do not reject it. (He looks askance at people who misjudge the time because of the way they are feeling. Why don't they look at their watch?)

Though imagination can lead us astray, it can also widen our perception of our condition. As a bleak metaphor for existence, Pascal writes in 434: 'Imagine a group of men in chains, condemned to death and to see the slaughter daily of each one, knowing their turn will come.' There are a number of other *Pensées* where Pascal appears to be stretching the imaginative powers of his reader. 427 is a lengthy passage which presents the dark drama of our place in the universe: 'Infinities on all sides, surrounding us like an atom, like a shadow that lasts only for an instant and returns no more.'

Imagining ultimate goodness, imagining God in his almighty power is not something Pascal asks of his readers but, with St Paul, he encourages us to identify with what is good and of good report. 'Only the heart is able to receive God,' Pascal repeats, but we are left to find the faculties most suited to our own quest.

MIGHT AND RIGHT

Imagination, stretching to conceptualise Almighty
Fixes on boldest strength and infinite power,
And calls this Might.

In search of righteousness, opts for purest good
With deepest truth
And calls this Right
Then, with distillation of these both,
Barbs arrows which, like Cupid's dart,
Will pierce a torpid world, and this,
The arrow's flight,
We will call Love.

So, stretch the mind as eyes are stretched
To still more distant peaks.
Encourage daring leaps.
Outstride the pedestrian,
Duck the restricting bar.
But, if solid fact is there
And you avert your eyes,
The wise will watch with baleful eyes
And forecast your demise.

2 1

REFLECTIONS

A s has been seen, Pascal's style reflects his message. Brunschvicg labels section 1 of his classification 'Sur l'esprit et sur le style'. Antithesis, paradox, repetition, reflection characterise the human condition, as they do the natural world, and perhaps what lies beyond it. Ideas variously expressed concur and provide a spotlight of vision in the same way as the senses receive different but consistent images of nature's glory, and the promise of life to come.

Centuries before Darwin, Pascal was fascinated by the interweaving of repetition and variety in the material world. In *Pensée* 663 he writes: 'Finite objects multiply indefinitely, infinitely … It seems to me that the number which multiplies them is infinite.' Then, with an even more modern ring: 'Infinity appears more as a law of the mind which makes the calculations than a property of the universe. In theory, everything is divisible or multipliable.' We find that, like the many sides of a cut diamond, Pascal's thoughts reappear in slightly different colours, reverberate like the diapason stop of an organ pipe, rebound off one another. He recognises that this characterises no less the equivocation that results in an age of uncertainty and moral relativism.

Reflect!

Reflections offer much to wonder at.
Lakeside shots showing
Swans' necks protruding down,
Butterflies with four wings.
And those sunsets!
Glory doubled over water.
And then the crazy angled mirrors
(Images ricocheted to infinity),
No less, untamed rebounding of thought between
Nailed down notions.
So that all can seem insubstantial,
Reversible, upturnable.
Save for the stay of faith that
Since we have drunk deep
Of earth's multiplication,
We may, while still in the reverberation
Of death's diapason,
Feel the reflected glory of the Risen Lord,
And glimpse an infinity of angels' wings.

22

POSTLUDE (ETERNITY)

PASCAL COULD NOT EXPECT HIS WOULD-BE CONVERT to experience the blinding revelation that he had experienced on that November night in 1654. Nor did the seventeenth-century mind, still fed on medieval images of heaven and hell, regularly produce intimations of immortality such as we find expressed in poetry of later centuries. For Pascal, immortality was the consequence of a life well lived, and eternity the promise given to those who have been mindful of it. There are some who may be unexpected recipients.

Candle

Just one candle stands lit
(On a holder built for twenty).
Its flame is wan and sorry
In the blazing sun.
'Who put it there?'
No clues from an empty church.
One thinks of a frail old lady dressed in black,
Remembering her dead.
One imagines her fumbling for matches,
For her coin, and the slot to put it in.
But see, instead, the apologetic gesture
Of a thick-set man, more often seen in a football ground,
Or in a bar, who, feeling there must be something to explain
The woeful here and now, slips, unnoticed, he hopes,
    into a church,
Applies a smoker's light,
Slips the candle into the holder
With the confidence of one changing a light bulb
And claims the existence of eternity.

In other instances, it is precisely the non-fulfilment of earthly aspirations that provides the brush with the eternal. Pascal implies that it is a matter of maintaining a vision of eternity to which one may direct one's life. In *Pensée* 429, in which he voices a friend's discomfort in a troubling world, he has him say 'My whole heart strains to know what is the true good in order to pursue it. No price would be too high to pay for eternity.'

Precious the path denied.
The path ahead, you will recall, invites.
The tread is wide and grassy,
Bosky edged with primroses beside.
Our mutual soul leapt forward,
But our limbs were stayed:
A barbed wire obstacle our way denied.
How many times this image comes to me,
When disappointment strikes with barb or thorn.
It was the loveliest path, the fondest hope
Which now is gone.

If human life must always know such blocks,
Such hindrance, confrontation, thwarted hope,
I'll play the game of faith
And yearn for immortality:
The unimpeded path straight through eternity;
The arrow's flight path to infinity.

Pascal expresses his passionate conviction that eternity offers something infinitely finer than anything that can be experienced on earth.

What price eternity?

What price eternity?
What is priceless is
The wholesome wholing of failed aspirations;
The salving of, balming of, smarting frustrations.
Glimpses of God given total fruition.
(Hearts thus fulfilling their truest ambition.)
Hopes, dreams and visions now reignited.
Despairing dashed and love requited.

In Section VII, 'Divertissement' (or 'Diversion'), he rehearses humanity's failed attempts to find happiness, fulfilment, satisfaction of any kind. He observes that we are taught from an early age to give our time to promoting health, wealth, reputation – our own and that of friends and family. A lack in any of these areas will make us unhappy. Pascal recognises that those who have found happiness have followed a different code. In *Pensées* 27–29, he studies the life of Saint Teresa of Avila.

All have witnessed, as did Pascal, that the death of those whose life seemed blameless appears as a natural transition into another realm, for which they were more fitted.

IF A CHARIOT SHOULD FETCH THEM

If a chariot should fetch them,
Swung low,
Those tried in the fire
And not found wanting.
If a chariot should graze the lower reaches
To take them back,
It is to rest their weary feet, dusty and sore
From untended, lengthy roads;
Their shoulders bent with
Cares of a world uncaring;
Their eyes straining for vision
In a clouded, tawdry age.

Would Pascal have given thought to the possibility of communication between heaven and earth? Probably not. In spite of the prominent position given to the Incarnation in his theology, it seems unlikely that, beyond the doctrine of 'communion of saints', he would have approved of this sort of speculation. In *Pensée* 927, however, he considers the interrelation of all created things. 'The slightest movement affects the whole world; the entire ocean can change because of a stone.'

MARCH 2011

May we consider that earth's quakes disturb the heavens?
That if repentant sinners fill the vault with joy,
And fears and tears below distress divinity,
Then, surely, devastation of their one-time home
Must shake the slumbers of the newly dead.
Surely Koji, long-bearded, weeps
To see his ruined country,
And longs to take his orphaned grandchild
In his arms.
Theology apart: If they say a bee's demise
Can cause a flood a thousand miles away,
We do not need to look beyond the stars
To estimate a trembling caused by earthly scars.

Two-way sacrament?

Those who, flesh cast aside, now live in spirit free,
In realms of light where saints rejoiced at the Nativity,
Rejoice again as God presents as bread
And know the veil is rent between the living and the dead.
May you now glimpse the life you knew?
Faces, a place, a favoured view?
Glimpse once again the things that you held dear?
If so, is it permitted that I feel you near?

Mostly our concept of eternity can only be constructed with what is unearthly, not of earth. We sense in many of the *Pensées* that Pascal feels ashamed that humanity can stoop so low, can show disregard for the majesty of creation; that we are more concerned to impress others than to benefit from God's munificence. Maybe eternity can be imagined only by rejecting with horror, as Pascal does, repugnant behaviour and our own self-centredness.

The globe of eternity's glorious otherness:
No crack, fissure, leak,
Fracture or break.
No worm holes, black holes,
Black matter.
Because, gloriously,
No matter.

Trinity Sunday

Newspaper headline: 'Man fined for urinating in church font.'

Thank God, eternity's devoid of human waste,
And heaven needs no font to send its blessings down.
The Sistine spark is passed forever round:
Divine recycling,
With breath breathed out from breath to breath,
Drawn from the fount of love.

The unknown breadth;
Sole, forever breath
(Which is both giving and receiving).
Here we both are
And are not
(As a soap bubble both is and is not),
Where we live as light
And glimpse our little time and space
As a distant dewdrop on a ghostly rose.

GLIMPSING ETERNITY?

In the quiet, dark reaches of the night,
I, like one taking a sample of earth,
Carved out what felt like eternity
As a lightning flash
Both deafeningly loud and startlingly still,
Unmeasured breadth, unfathomed depth,
Unthinkably vast, unthinkably small
And, once perceived, not there at all.

A MUSICIAN MEDITATES ON THE MUSIC OF THE SPHERES

See to it that nothing suggests mortality.
No cadences, no dying fall.
(They could segment the seamless weave.)
No fugue or sequence which the minds tease out;
The heart must rule where soul attends.
Let it be loud to herald nature's birth,
But soft in whispering its mystery.
Fast for excitement of being,
But slow to take in the meaning.
Minor for man's sad mess of things,
But major for his redemption.
In triple time for unity
(But steering clear of waltz or minuet).
And in what key?
Here, like those at the first Pentecost,
We may both hear and see
Our favourite key.

Pascal does not disregard the importance of 'our brief duration', but he regrets that the precious human gifts of space and time are so often wasted. 'Since the present never satisfies us, experience tricks us, leads us from misfortune to misfortune until death.' Only the heart knows a different and secret path.

TIME

Time
Surrendered to sleep,
Squandered, snatched for indulgence,
Meted out for obligation,
This we gladly forfeit.
But, ah, sublimated time
Which stops the clock's hand,
And the mind's calculation
As a leaf dallies in descent
And the robin's vermilion song
Reflects the sun's last rays
In an autumn evening
That spells its own eternity.

SPACE

Our Archimedes principle and privilege.
The space to swing a cat;
To draw a bow;
Or make a bow.
Thus to express our personality;
Define our frontiers.
The space we call our own
(Cultivated familiarity).
But then, the space the coffin leaves behind,
The pictured space behind unanswered telephones.
This we might leave behind.

But, ah, sequestrated space!
Where rabbits play under oaks at a river's bend,
Where wild thyme grows.
This spells its immortality.

Pensée 399 asks two pertinent questions: 'If Man is not made for God, why is it that he finds happiness nowhere else?' and 'If Man is made for God, why does he so oppose Him?' In 618 Pascal concludes: 'If there is a God, we must love Him.' Only once does Pascal record a feeling of personal happiness. The eleventh line of the Memorial reads; 'Joie, joie, pleurs de joie [joy, joy, tears of joy]'. Elsewhere it is more a question of observing the unhappiness suffered by most of the human race, despite every attempt to avoid it. We are, nonetheless, made for happiness, and it constitutes our perennial goal and ambition, but eludes us constantly. 'La félicité est en Lui seul [Happiness is in Him alone].'

Section X, 'Thoughts on the Sovereign Good', opens with a quotation from Seneca. 'That you may be content in yourself and with good things innate in you.' The desire for happiness is 'the motive of every man, including those who go and hang themselves'. Pascal finds this craving proves that 'there was once in Man true happiness, but of which all that remains is the empty print and trace' (*Pensée* 147). In 148, he gives a strange list of things that have been tried to replace it: 'Stars, sky, earth, elements, plants, cabbages, leeks, animals, insects, serpents, calves, fever, plague, war, famine, vice, adultery, incest.' And later: 'Authority, intellectual enquiry, knowledge, pleasure.' But he insists that the infinite abyss we experience once happiness has left 'can be filled only with an infinite and immutable object'. In other words, by God himself. This he offers as the prize to be gained in eternity.

Pascal's wealthy friends, already aiming to stifle serious thought by means of constant activity and diversion, were unlikely to welcome the idea of a static heaven where joy is to be defined as the beatific contemplation of the Godhead. Pascal, whose religious fervour was further strengthened by the mathematical belief that infinity finds its resolution in God, would have felt, as the writer of the English hymn,

> Content before Thy throne to lie
> And gaze and gaze on Thee.

A prize not worth the winning?
A prospect truly chilling?
But, if there be not eyes to tire?
And if the mind knows no fatigue?
No thoughts to bore,
No 'déjà vu'
No 'toujours su',
But all is new
Complete to view,
Then may I wish, most sovereign God
To gaze on you.

Pascal is reluctant to write about eternity, even though he does not doubt its existence. Ariew's translation from the Sellier edition (see Chapter 9) helps us to understand why: 'We know the existence of the infinite, but we do not know its nature, because it has extension like us, but not limits like us' (from translation of Sellier 680). Pascal prefers to stay with mathematics: 'Numbers follow one another from beginning to end. Thus is created a kind of infinity and eternity. Not that anything in all this is infinite or eternal, but these finite things are infinitely multiplied.' Once again, we meet the belief that the human mind is not made for knowing everything.

'Too much knowledge leads to pride, too little to despair' (*Pensée* 199, as paraphrased earlier). A number of the *Pensées* speak of the *juste milieu*, the happy medium which most suits our condition. Quoting further from Ariew's translation: 'The eternity of things in themselves or in God must always astonish our brief duration; what is more, our complicated nature prevents us from seeing what may ultimately be simple. Instead of receiving the ideas in their purity, we taint them with our own qualities and stamp our composite being on all the simple things we contemplate.'

This does not prevent present-day speculation. Modern cosmology offers the possibility of parallel universes. Theologians too. Keith Ward in

Pascal's Fire addresses this possibility.[1] One cannot guess whether Pascal would have subscribed to this. He pondered (*Pensée* 571) the significance of 'omnes [all men]' in relation to salvation, not sharing the Jansenist position that heaven was reserved for a select few. That we might find at death that there is a second chance of getting things right is a tempting thought.

PARALLEL WORLDS

A tempting thought for those of us
Who missed the boat, took a wrong turn,
Or simply made a gaffe.
That other me out there,
Enjoying wealth, success,
Or maybe even happiness.
Better by far than pie in the sky
This unearned beatitude,
Where we can ask a good and gentle God
To harvest all that makes the grade,
And cancel out our punier selves
(Like crooked teeth or falling shares,
Aborted foetuses).
And Judas's betrayal? Adam's 'happy fault'?
I like to think that heaven boasts a higher goal,
Where all the strange and fascinating forms
Of nature's malformation
Are taken in with love,
Sanctified.

---

1 Pages 36–8, 243–4.

REFERENCES AND
FURTHER READING

(In French)

Lafuma, Louis, *Pascal: Œuvres complètes*, Éditions du Seuil (Collection Integrale), 1963

Brunschvicg, Léon, *Pascal, Pensées et opuscules*, Hachette, first published 1897

Mesnard, Jean, *Les Pensées de Pascal*, SEDES, 1976

(In English)

Ariew, Roger, *Blaise Pascal: Pensées*, Hackett, 2005

Cruickshank, John, *Pascal Pensées* (*Critical Guides to French Texts*), Grant and Cutler, 1983

Daniel-Rops, Henri, *The Church in the Seventeenth Century*, Dent & Son, 1963

Devlin, Keith, *The Unfinished Game: Pascal, Fermat, and the Seventeenth-Century Letter that Made the World Modern*, Perseus, 2008

Eastwood, D.M., *The Revival of Pascal*, Clarendon Press, 1936

Krailsheimer, Alban, *Blaise Pascal: Pensées*, Penguin Classics, revised edn, 1995

Krailsheimer, Alban, *Pascal* (*Past Masters*), Oxford University Press, 1980

Kreeft, Peter, *Christianity for Modern Pagans*, Ignatius, 1993

Steinmann, Jean, *Pascal* (trans. Martin Turnell), Burns & Oates, 1965

Treasure, Geoffrey, *Seventeenth Century France*, John Murray, 1970, reprinted 1984

Turnell, Martin, *Pascal's Pensées*, Harvill, 1962

Ward, Keith, *Pascal's Fire: Scientific Faith and Religious Understanding*, Oneworld Books, 2006

FURTHER READING

Connor, James A., *Pascal's Wager: The Man Who Played Dice with God*, Harper San Francisco, 2006 [A fascinating account which offers a very different slant on Pascal's character and life]

Devlin, Keith, *Goodbye, Descartes: The End of Logic and the Search for a New Cosmology of the Mind*, John Wiley and Sons, 1998

Gilbert, Peter Brian, *Pascal's God-shaped Vacuum*, CreateSpace, 2012

Jordan, Jeff, *Gambling on God: Essays on Pascal's Wager*, Rowman and Littlefield, 1994

Krailsheimer, Alban, *Blaise Pascal: Human Happiness*, Penguin (Great Ideas), 2009 [A pleasing short collection from Krailsheimer's own translation]

Treasure, Geoffrey, *The Huguenots*, Yale University Press, 2013

Van de Weyer, Roger, *Pascal in a Nutshell*, Hodder & Stoughton, 1997 [A personal selection of a devotional nature, ending with 'For the Use of Sickness', material from, though not identified as, 'The Mystery of Jesus']

TOPICAL INDEX
TO THE *PENSÉES*

Selective index to the topics presented in the *Pensées*, listed alphabetically according to Krailsheimer's classification. Numbers in **bold** indicate *Pensées* that have been given particular attention in the text or poems.